HOLIDAY FAVORITES

Solos and Band Arrangements
Correlated with Essential Elements® Band Method

Arranged by ROBERT LONGFIELD, JOHNNIE VINSON, MICHAEL SWEENEY and PAUL LAVENDER

Welcome to Essential Elements Holiday Favorites! There are two versions of each selection in this versatile book. The SOLO version appears in the beginning of each student book. The FULL BAND arrangement of each song follows. The ONLINE RECORDINGS or PIANO ACCOMPANIMENT BOOK may be used as an accompaniment for solo performance. Use these recordings when playing solos for friends and family.

PLAYBACK+
Speed • Pitch • Balance • Loop

To access audio visit:
www.halleonard.com/mylibrary

Enter Code
4733-4685-8216-5064

ISBN 978-1-5400-2799-3

00870017

Visit Hal Leonard Online at
www.halleonard.com

Contact Us:
Hal Leonard
7777 West Bluemound Road
Milwaukee, WI 53213
Email: info@halleonard.com

In Europe contact:
Hal Leonard Europe Limited
42 Wigmore Street
Marylebone, London, W1U 2RN
Email: info@halleonardeurope.com

In Australia contact:
Hal Leonard Australia Pty. Ltd.
4 Lentara Court
Cheltenham, Victoria, 3192 Australia
Email: info@halleonard.com.au

T0055839

AULD LANG SYNE

BARITONE T.C.
Solo

Words by ROBERT BURNS
Traditional Scottish Melody
Arranged by MICHAEL SWEENEY

FELIZ NAVIDAD

BARITONE T.C.
Solo

Music and Lyrics by
JOSÉ FELICIANO
Arranged by PAUL LAVENDER

00870017

PARADE OF THE WOODEN SOLDIERS

BARITONE T.C.
Solo

English Lyrics by BALLARD MacDONALD
Music by LEON JESSEL
Arranged by PAUL LAVENDER

Toy March

GOOD KING WENCESLAS

BARITONE T.C.
Solo

Words by JOHN M. NEALE
Music from PIAE CANTIONES
Arranged by ROBERT LONGFIELD

PAT-A-PAN
(Willie, Take Your Little Drum)

BARITONE T.C.
Solo

Words and Music by
BERNARD de la MONNOYE
Arranged by ROBERT LONGFIELD

SILVER BELLS

BARITONE T.C.
Solo

Words and Music by
JAY LIVINGSTON and RAY EVANS
Arranged by PAUL LAVENDER

00870017

DO YOU HEAR WHAT I HEAR

BARITONE T.C.
Solo

Words and Music by
NOEL REGNEY and GLORIA SHAYNE
Arranged by MICHAEL SWEENEY

Moderately

From THE SOUND OF MUSIC

MY FAVORITE THINGS

BARITONE T.C.
Solo

Lyrics by OSCAR HAMMERSTEIN II
Music by RICHARD RODGERS
Arranged by ROBERT LONGFIELD

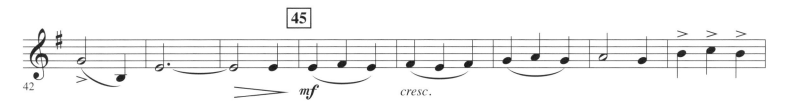

From the Motion Picture Irving Berlin's HOLIDAY INN

WHITE CHRISTMAS

BARITONE T.C.
Solo

**Words and Music by
IRVING BERLIN**
Arranged by JOHNNIE VINSON

CHRISTMAS TIME IS HERE

BARITONE T.C.
Solo

Words by LEE MENDELSON
Music by VINCE GUARALDI
Arranged by JOHNNIE VINSON

From Warner Bros. Pictures' THE POLAR EXPRESS

THE POLAR EXPRESS

BARITONE T.C.
Solo

Words and Music by
GLEN BALLARD and **ALAN SILVESTRI**
Arranged by JOHNNIE VINSON

Moderately Fast

AULD LANG SYNE

BARITONE T.C.
Band Arrangement

Words by ROBERT BURNS
Traditional Scottish Melody
Arranged by MICHAEL SWEENEY

00870017

FELIZ NAVIDAD

BARITONE T.C.
Band Arrangement

Music and Lyrics by
JOSÉ FELICIANO
Arranged by PAUL LAVENDER

PARADE OF THE WOODEN SOLDIERS

BARITONE T.C.
Band Arrangement

English Lyrics by BALLARD MacDONALD
Music by LEON JESSEL
Arranged by PAUL LAVENDER

GOOD KING WENCESLAS

BARITONE T.C.
Band Arrangement

Words by JOHN M. NEALE
Music from PIAE CANTIONES
Arranged by ROBERT LONGFIELD

Moderato

PAT-A-PAN
(Willie, Take Your Little Drum)

BARITONE T.C.
Band Arrangement

Words and Music by
BERNARD de la MONNOYE
Arranged by ROBERT LONGFIELD

SILVER BELLS

BARITONE T.C.
Band Arrangement

Words and Music by
JAY LIVINGSTON and RAY EVANS
Arranged by PAUL LAVENDER

DO YOU HEAR WHAT I HEAR

BARITONE T.C.
Band Arrangement

Words and Music by
NOEL REGNEY and **GLORIA SHAYNE**
Arranged by MICHAEL SWEENEY

From THE SOUND OF MUSIC

MY FAVORITE THINGS

BARITONE T.C.
Band Arrangement

Lyrics by **OSCAR HAMMERSTEIN II**
Music by **Richard Rodgers**
Arranged by ROBERT LONGFIELD

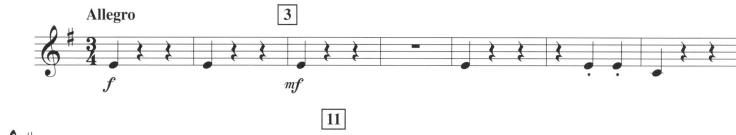

From the Motion Picture Irving Berlin's HOLIDAY INN

WHITE CHRISTMAS

BARITONE T.C.
Band Arrangement

Words and Music by
IRVING BERLIN
Arranged by JOHNNIE VINSON

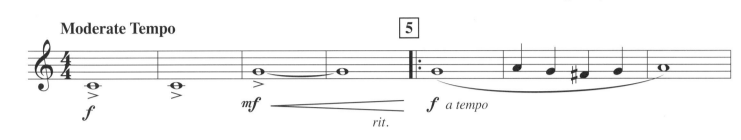

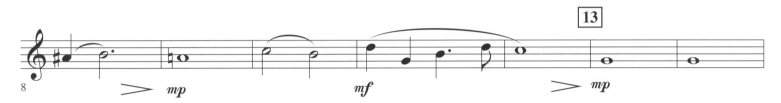

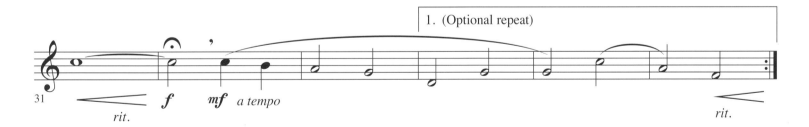

00870017

CHRISTMAS TIME IS HERE

BARITONE T.C.
Band Arrangement

Words by LEE MENDELSON
Music by VINCE GUARALDI
Arranged by JOHNNIE VINSON

THE POLAR EXPRESS

BARITONE T.C.
Band Arrangement

Words and Music by
GLEN BALLARD and **ALAN SILVESTRI**
Arranged by JOHNNIE VINSON